For everyone who has ever been on a bug hunt: May you always find adventure in your own backyard! -C.M.J.

Layout and design by Carla Mae Jansen.

www.TurtleTrailsPublishing.com

Can you find this squirrel in 12 spots throughout the book?

When Will CICADA Sing?

Carla Mae Jansen

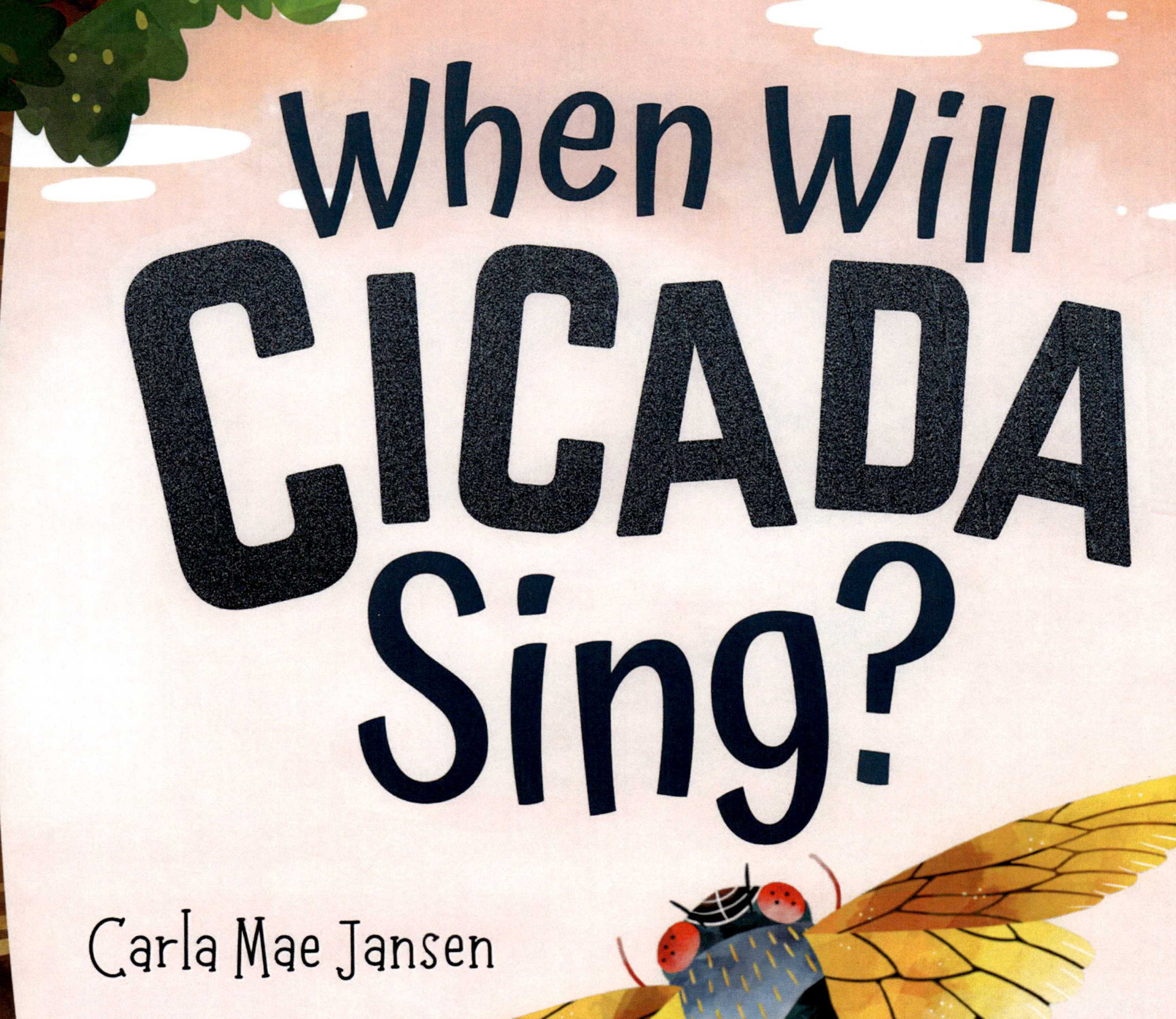

Cicada started life as

a tiny egg

tucked in a crack on a tree.

Would he sing?

Not today.

Eggs do not sing.

No crawling or drinking or playing, it's true,

And he couldn't sing yet--he had growing to do.

Fifty days came and passed, and Cicada's egg cracked open.

He was a **nymph**.

Would he sing now?

No. Tiny baby cicadas do not sing.

He fell to the ground,
crawled under the dirt, and slept.

The next day he poked a small hole in the roots and drank sap from a tree.

Yum, yum, yum!

He crawled, and he drank,
and he slept, and he grew.

But he couldn't sing yet--
he had growing to do!

More days came and passed.

Cold air fell on the forest.

Cicada burrowed deeper, where the soil was warmer.

He crawled, and he drank,
and he slept, and he grew.

But he couldn't sing yet--
he had growing to do!

One day, he had grown so much that his small shell squished his body.

He molted his old shell, and crawled out, a little **bigger**!

Years came and passed. Cicada grew so much that he molted three more times!

He was more than ten times bigger than when he first climbed out of his egg, but he stayed underground.

He crawled, and he drank,
and he slept, and he grew.

But he couldn't sing yet--
he had growing to do!

Finally,
seventeen
winters
came
and passed.

The ground was warm.

Cicada knew it was time to climb back out of the dirt.

Sunshine hit his face for the first time in seventeen years!

His shell squished his growing body again. He needed to molt one last time.

Cicada climbed up a tall tree and held tightly to its bark. He pushed through his old shell until it cracked open.

He climbed out, and he stretched his fully-grown wings.

Would he sing now?

Soon! So soon!

First he needed to hide somewhere safe while his new shell hardened.

A few days later his shell was hard, and the sun warmed his whole body.

It was time to sing!

He heard dozens of other cicadas singing in the trees, and he climbed to join them.

He climbed, and he crawled,
and he stretched himself too.

He was ready for this--
he had singing to do!

His strong tymbals beat like a drum, making a song that grew louder and louder. He beat his tymbals faster and faster...

100 times a second,

200 times a second,

300 times a second!

His song buzzed louder than anything else in the forest!

Soon another cicada landed on the tree next to him.

She looked at him, and he knew that the seventeen years of waiting were about to start all over again for a new generation of cicadas--

--a new generation of cicadas that were about to begin life as little eggs tucked inside a crack in a tree.

17-Year Cicada Life Cycle

ADULT

- Lives 4-6 weeks
- Eats tree sap
- Males "sing" to attract females
- Lays eggs

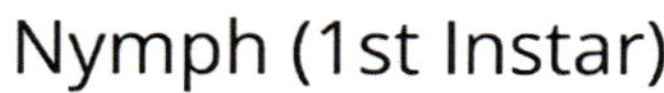

Nymph (1st Instar)

- Crawls underground
- Eats sap
- Burrows

EGGS

- Laid in bark on branches
- Up to 20 eggs laid at once
- Hatch in 6-10 weeks

Nymph (2nd Instar)

- Lives underground
- Eats sap
- Burrows

Nymph (3rd Instar)

- Lives underground
- Eats sap
- Burrows

Nymph (4th Instar)

- Lives underground
- Eats sap
- Burrows

Nymph (5th Instar)

- Crawls above ground
- Eats sap
- Has many predators

How Do Cicadas Sing?

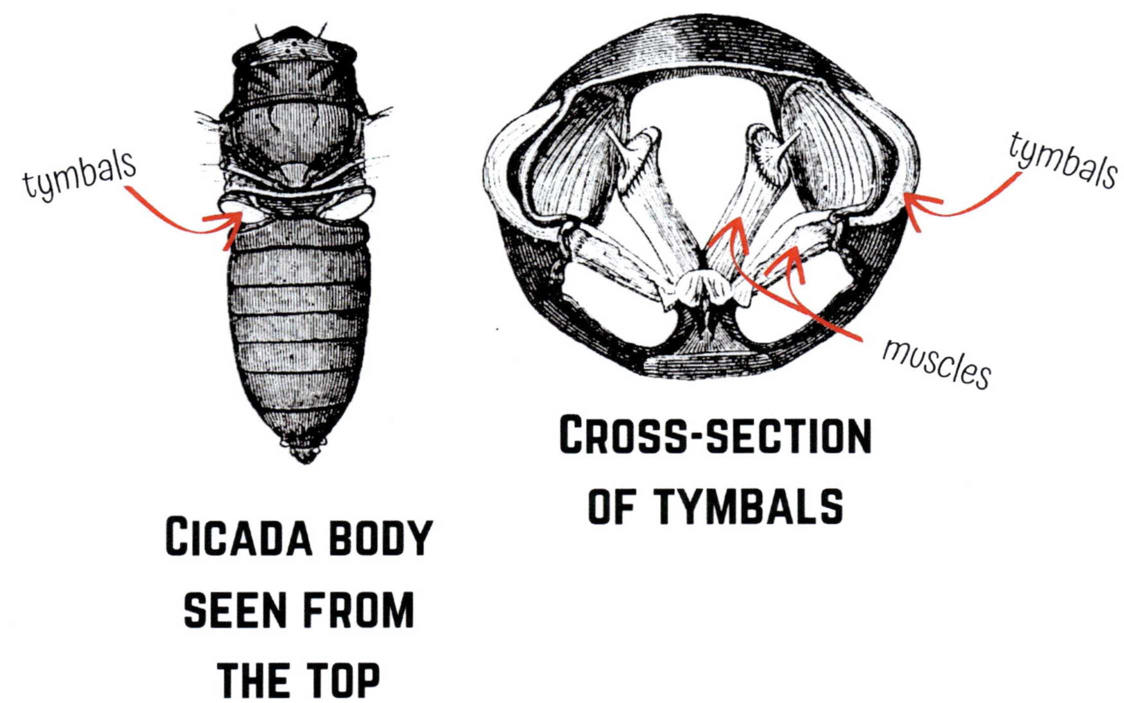

Male cicadas have tymbals that act like a drum top. When muscles pull the tymbals in, they makes a buzz sound. When the muscles release the tymbals, they snap back into place and buzz again.

When cicadas beat those muscles hundreds of times every second, the sounds echo together and get louder!

Meet the Author:

Carla Mae Jansen loves finding cool insects and learning about them! She also loves mountains, rocks, and ice-cream!

She is a mom, teacher (MA Science Education), and author. Email her at Carla@TurtleTrailsPublishing.com.

Also by the Author:

A Dinosaur Made Me Sneeze: A Rock Cycle Adventure is the award-winning tale of how dinosaurs started a chain reaction that lasted for millions of years! Outrageous sneezes, volcanoes, the rock cycle, and a crazy skink are just a part of the fun!

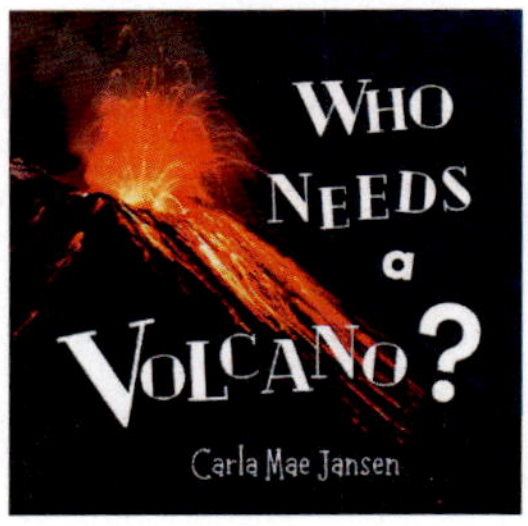

Who Needs a Volcano? is the highly-acclaimed non-fiction picture book that introduces our youngest readers to animals that actually use volcanoes in surprising and practical ways!

Did you love this book? Please leave a review!

Made in United States
North Haven, CT
23 January 2024